The ABISHAI Anointing

DENNY DURON

Library of Congress: TXu-1-046-875

ISBN: 0-9722562-2-9

This book was printed in the United States of America.

To order additional copies of this book, contact:
Denny Duron Evangelistic Assosication
1-800-403-4150
www.dennyduron.org

Cover art by Dave Ivey

DEDICATION

To my beautiful wife DeAnza
and our six precious gifts from God:
Destiny, DawnCheré, Denny Rodney,
Dez, David Dee, and Dakota

Table of Contents

1

THE MISSING ANOINTING

David was a man after God's own heart. He is one of history's most fascinating leaders– a warrior poet, a musician general, a shepherd king. David, a legend bigger than life, as a boy slew a bear and a lion and then wasted a nine-foot killing machine named Goliath with a single shot from his sling. David's psalms were sung each Sabbath by the temple worship team. He brought the ark of presence back to Jerusalem and danced wildly in worship as the entourage entered the gates. The David anointing is the anointing of God's visionary, God's point person. This is a man or woman who is not afraid to make the tough decisions.

This is a person who spends time with God and declares His word to the people. We are always in desperate need of the David anointing.

We must have contemporary Davids who will face the giants of secularism, apostasy, and error that now challenge the church. We must have those who will restore the art of worship and will bring back the priority of the manifest presence of God. Why aren't there more David anointings today? I believe it is because another vital anointing is missing.

This missing anointing is seldom mentioned, but it is of paramount importance. It is the anointing of mighty men and women to stand with the leader who is called of God. These people are not Davids and do not aspire to be, but they have an anointing that releases and empowers God's man or woman to fulfill God's calling. This is the Abishai Anointing.

2

EXTRAORDINARY
FOR THE ORDINARY

ABISHAI, the brother of Joab, the son of Zeruiah, was chief of the thirty. And he swung his spear against three hundred and killed them, and had a name as well as the three.

He was most honored of the thirty, therefore he became their commander; however, he did not attain to three.

(II SAMUEL 23:18-19 NASB)

Abishai was David's nephew, the son of David's sister, Zeruiah. He was more honorable than some. The Bible says he was the captain of thirty of David's mighty men. He was less honorable than others. He did not attain the status of the three senior commanders of David's elite fighters. Abishai is just like those God is looking for – ordinary men and women with an extraordinary anointing. This anointing belongs to those in the middle of the pack who are more honorable than some and less honorable than others.

In Alan Redpath's classic book, *The Making of a Man of God*, he states, "Sometimes we covet attractive and talented people for the Lord's work...The basis of God's choice is contrary to all this – when He would build a "man of God" He looks for different timber." The Bible says in I Corinthians 1:27-29: *"God hath chosen the foolish things of the world to confound the wise...the weak things of the world to confound the things which are mighty; And base things...and things which are despised, hath God chosen, yea, and things which are not, to bring to nought things that are: That no flesh should glory in his presence" (KJV).*

Abishai is just one among a delta force of heroes chronicled in scripture, yet no one exemplifies this special empowering servant spirit like this man. This is what I call the Abishai Anointing, a vital scriptural anointing.

3

BORN IN TOUGH TIMES

SO David departed from there and escaped to the cave of Adullam; and when his brothers and all his father's household heard of it, they went down there to him.

Everyone who was in distress, and everyone who was in debt, and everyone who was discontented gathered to him; and he became captain over them. Now there were about four hundred men with him.

(I Samuel 22:1-2 NASB)

The Abishai Anointing is an anointing that is born in tough times. David had a price on his head. He was a fugitive, running for his life. He and his guerilla band chose a cave at Adullam for their camp and base of operations. The Bible says all who were discouraged and distressed and in debt came to Adullam. The church that Abishai joined at Adullam was neither the fastest growing, nor the most talked about. It was the First Church of the Discouraged, Distressed and in Debt. Abishai, along with his mom and two brothers, made his way to the campfires of the cave of Adullam knowing there would be no personal guarantees of comfort, security, position, prestige, or recognition. That was just fine. They had not come for what they could receive, but rather they had come for what they could give to their outcast king.

How different those revolutionaries at Adullam were from the fair-weather followers of today. In America, our twenty-first century version of Christianity is not about "the cause," "the cross," or "the King." It is about us. If we and our family can get a better deal, then we abandon leadership at Adullam and head for a place of ease. But not Abishai, for his anointing was born in tough times.

Vince Lombardi, a NFL Hall of Fame coach, said, "When the going gets tough, the tough get going!"

The ABISHAI Anointing

For the most part, today we would have to coin a new slogan: when the going gets tough, many Christians go away.

> THEY GO AWAY **OFFENDED.**
> THEY GO AWAY **HURT.**
> THEY GO AWAY **CRITICAL.**
> THEY GO AWAY **COMPLAINING.**

They go away forfeiting the Abishai Anointing and an opportunity to be a part of something greater than themselves.

It has often been said you can tell the level of one's commitment by what makes him or her quit!

In today's "please me" generation, most Christians abandon their leadership because they are personally offended. It doesn't take much of a trial or a disappointment – just something small, to make them abandon ship. No wonder Jesus always wanted it understood up front what He demanded.

> *THEN Jesus said to His disciples, If anyone wishes to come after Me, he must deny himself, and take up his cross and follow Me.*

For whoever wishes to save his life will lose it; but whoever loses his life for My sake will find it.
(MATTHEW 16:24-25 NASB)

A pastor sees so few Abishais in his congregation. However, the few that are there, whose anointing was born in tough times, are the ones he knows will stand with him in the Adullams ahead.

A dimension of anointing exists that only comes when you are willing to share the burden as well as the blessing of leadership. The Bible says, *"If we endure, we will also reign with Him..."* (II Timothy 2:12 NASB). Jesus did not call His disciples to a king's table or an earthly palace. He could have done that. He chose not to. He called them to the Adullam of His rejection, suffering, and lack; but He knew that if they were willing to commit there, the kingdoms and the kings of this world would be no match for their power, their authority, and their anointing. Abishais, like Peter, James, and John, turned the world upside down because they had an anointing that was born in tough times.

The ABISHAI Anointing

In the early 1970s, I preached regularly in New York City at Calvary Tabernacle in Brooklyn. This thriving, powerful inner-city work was pastored by a man who became a mentor and close friend of mine – Dr. Ben Crandall. Each service in Calvary Temple was energized by ethnicity. It was an all-nations church and the combination of worship styles was pure delight. I often wondered as I sat listening to the large multicultural choir and looking out over a packed sanctuary – where did this great anointing begin?

Some of my most treasured moments were when Dr. Crandall would drive me through the city and, in his own quiet, piercing way, spend time speaking truth into my life. One day in front of an old abandoned building in a slum area, tears filled Ben's eyes as he pointed to the crumbling structure under an elevated traintrack. He said, "Denny, that's where we started forty years ago. I was fresh out of Bible school. We set chairs in that old building and had church every night for months. I slept on the floor of that rat-infested place. That's where it all began." I suddenly understood the glory of God that resided in Calvary Tabernacle. This was an anointing born in tough times.

An unusually large group of elders and deacons served in the congregation and their love for their pastor was obvious. Dr. Crandall informed me that this innercircle of comrades had been with him almost from the beginning. Those who now stood in the crowded sanctuary as deacons and elders also remembered where it all began. They had joined themselves to a young man who had nothing but a vision, and their commitment to an Adullam experience brought the awesome approval of Almighty God.

4

I WILL GO WITH YOU

DAVID then arose and came to the place where Saul had camped. And David saw the place where Saul lay, and Abner the son of Ner, the commander of his army; and Saul was lying in the circle of the camp, and the people were camped around him.

Then David said to Ahimelech the Hittitie and to Abishai the son of Zeuriah, Joab's brother, saying, "Who will go down with me to Saul in the camp?" And Abishai said, "I will go down with you."

(I SAMUEL 26:5-6 NASB)

David knows Saul is pursuing him to kill him, but his sense of adventure at this point begins to overtake his apprehension. He discovers exactly where Saul and his soldiers are camping and then goes back to Ahimelech and Abishai. I can hear Abishai say to Ahimelech as David aproaches: Uh-oh, he's got that 'Goliath look' on him again!

David says, boys, I know where they are. I'm sure they expected him to finish the statement by saying: Let's get out of here! Instead he says, who will go with me to the enemy's camp?

Now, Ahimelech was a Hittite, an Adullam mercenary, and fiercely loyal to David. However, he remains silent. I have known more than my share of Ahimelechs. Ahimelech is the Christian who knows theoretically that God works through faith in the realm of the miraculous, but he cannot personally move toward the vision of leadership. A pastor emerges from his time with God, and he has a vision of defying the odds and going to the enemy's camp in his city. He shares his heart, and one Ahimelech asks, can we afford it?

The ABISHAI Anointing

Another says, we've never done it that way before. The Ahimelechs are satisfied right where they are. They like being safe and secure. As Ahimelech sat in silence, Abishai, with no hesitation, answers, I'll go with you! Abishai had an advantage over Ahimelech. Since he was a youngster, he had sat at his mother's feet with his brothers and heard of Uncle David's exploits. He had heard how his Uncle David had beaten the odds and turned impossible situations into opportunities for God's miracles.

Abishai knew, just like Ahimelech, that in the natural this was a suicide mission. Just the two of them walking directly into the camp of Saul was insane. Saul was surrounded by three thousand troops and they were there to destroy David. The only strategy David had verbalized was: We're going right into the middle of the camp. Who wants to go with me? In spite of the odds, the danger, and the personal risk, Abishai cries, I'll go! That is the Abishai Anointing.

Abishai knew the glorious adventure of attacking the impossible with the anointed man of God. I believe that when we stand before the throne, we are going to give account of everything that was in our hearts. I am not referring to just evil motives, thoughts, and intents, though that is normally what comes into our minds. I believe we are also going to give account for every God-given dream, vision, and mission that the Ahimelechs talked us out of. Pastors, evangelists, and prophets are going to weep as they share their God-given dreams publicly for the very first time before the throne of Almighty God. Some will weep because they allowed the fearful, the practical, and logical advice of people around them to keep them from marching into the enemy's camp.

Even though each person must give account for himself, everyone needs a comrade. The scripture declares that one shall put a thousand to flight but two shall put ten thousand to flight, and that a three-ply cord cannot be easily broken.

Throughout history, where there is a David Anointing, behind the scenes there is always an Abishai or two – somebody who prayed, somebody who stayed in the tough times, and somebody who was always ready to go with the anointed leader.

5

TACKLING THE IMPOSSIBLE

I don't believe David would have gone to the enemy's camp alone or he would have gone immediately. He wanted somebody to go with him; somebody with that special anointing who is always ready to go. He needed an Abishai, who didn't ask how, when, where, or can we afford it? David desired an Abishai who was ready to go because he knew miracles happened when God's man or woman faced the challenge of overwhelming odds.

The thing that disturbs me about Christianity in the United States of America, is that we have reduced men and women of God to managing the norm, the boring, and the mundane. The general feeling of the church population seems to be, just give us our three songs, a sermon, and a benediction on Sunday mornings, and don't get any foolish ideas about breaking that pattern.

I have a dear friend named Rick Berlin. Rick has a heart for inner-city children. Some years ago we felt called by God to begin a camp for these high-risk children in our city. It was the Thursday before these camps were to begin on Monday when Rick came to me and said, "Denny, I've got everything organized. Now I would like to go buy the food for the camp."

"We don't have any money for food!" I said.

"What are we going to do? We've got to feed those children twice on Monday."

"We have to pray," I said.

Now, at a time like that, the Ahimelechs get very silent. You can hear their thoughts: I can't believe this guy. He should have thought of this before now. But this Abishai was ready to pray and believe God for the needs!

The ABISHAI Anointing

The next day I received a phone call from downtown. The unfamiliar voice on the line asked, "Mr. Duron? I heard you need some food. Well, I've got a truckload of food here and I would like to bring it over to you if you've got a freezer."

I said, "Yes sir, I've got a freezer here on my back porch, and I will clean it out to make room for the food you have. I certainly appreciate it."

He laughed and said, "You don't understand. It's not a pickup truck full of food. This is an eighteen wheeler full of food." He continued, "The strangest thing just happened. This truck driver was going through Shreveport on I-20, and his truck just turned over. Nobody's hurt, thank God, but we've got to do something with this food before it spoils. Do you have a big freezer?"

"Yes sir, I have a freezer."

"What's the address?"

"I don't know, but if you will call me back in five min-

23

utes, I'll tell you the address."

I knew that God was not going to provide an eighteen-wheeler full of food if he didn't intend to provide a freezer to put it in. My office manager, June Barnhill, called a local freezer company, and the owner of the company donated the space when he heard what we wanted to do with the food. When the man called back, I gave him the address and said, "Sir, before you get off the phone, would you mind telling me what's in the truck?"

"Oh, we've got steak fingers, chicken fingers, french fries…"

All the foods kids love! We fed our camps for two years from that truckload of food.

I am convinced Almighty God loves to see hearts joined together in a fervor of faith. He loves an Abishai who is willing to say, it's okay. We will just pray it in. If you want to go to the enemy's camp, I'm with you. I'm ready to go.

This is the Abishai Anointing!

6

COVENANT AGREEMENT

SO David and Abishai came to the people by night; and behold, Saul lay sleeping inside the circle of the camp with his spear stuck in the ground at his head; and Abner and the people were lying around him.

Then Abishai said to David, "Today God has delivered your enemy into your hand; now therefore, please, let me strike him with the spear to the ground with one stroke and I will not strike him the second time."

(I Samuel 26:7-8 NASB)

Saul had no grievance with David's nephew Abishai. He was not in line for the throne; only David was a threat.

Saul probably would have hired him as a mercenary if he had been given the chance. However, in I Samuel 26:8, we have a glimpse of Abishai's covenant heart. He wanted to kill David's enemy. Abishai was a covenant man. David's friends were his friends, and David's enemies were his enemies.

Jesus constantly spoke of covenant. The Bible is written in covenant language. Communion is a covenant ceremony of remembrance. The new birth is a covenant commitment. Discipleship is a covenant process. Covenant is all about total commitment and absolute loyalty! Jesus said, *"He who is not with Me is against Me; and he who does not gather with Me scatters"* (Matthew 12:30 NASB).

Jesus not only talks of commitment to God, but He also commands that we love our brothers as we love ourselves.

THE MESSAGE OF THE ABISHAI ANOINTING IS THAT WE REALLY DO NEED EACH OTHER.

The gospel is all about Christ loving people, caring for people, laying down His life for people, and shedding His covenant blood for people. The ministry of Christ called Him to know twelve men intimately and to give Himself to bearing their burdens, building their character, and interceding for their personal needs. The focus of today's Spirit-filled church is personal power, personal prosperity, personal success, and personal growth, but personal relationships are rare in the church and even more so among Christian leaders.

I spoke to a conference of ministers and asked, "How many of you have somebody you can tell anything to and know they will cover you, love you, tell you the truth, and keep your trust?"

Only one man in the room raised his hand. A generation of leaders who communicate a gospel of "ministry is more important than how you feel inside" are also destined to live under that same impersonal sentence of isolation. The reign of David was prosperous. During his reign the borders of Israel were secure, and his subjects were confident, but the crown of David's reign was his relationship with God and his glorious brothers.

A pastor shared with me how a staff member attacked him in front of his leadership team. This man spent over an hour accusing his leader, who sat silently. At the end of the young man's angry tirade, the pastor told the group that if what the man had said was true, he didn't need to be their pastor. The oldest member of his leadership team spoke first in response: Pastor, not one of us who walk with you believes any of these charges. This young man needs to leave. We're standing with you.

The Abishai Anointing stands against every enemy of his covenant partner. His leader is the delight of his heart and he honors him, protects him, and gladly fights for him in every conflict.

7

A TEACHABLE SPIRIT

As David and Abishai stood in the middle of Saul's regiment, Abishai's excitement spilled over. God had supernaturally put the whole fighting force of Saul into a deep sleep!

Abishai knew David. He understood that David was not interested in any action that did not have God's approval. So Abishai couched his comment in spiritual language:

> THEN Abishai said to David, "Today God has delivered your enemy into your hand"...But David said to Abishai, "Do not destroy him, for who can stretch out his hand against the LORD'S anointed

29

and be without guilt?"

David also said, "As the LORD lives, surely the LORD will strike him, or his day will come that he dies, or he will go down into battle and perish."

"The LORD forbid that I should stretch out my hand against the LORD'S anointed; but now please take the spear that is at his head and the jug of water, and let us go."

(I SAMUEL 26:8-11)

Abishai felt he had a word of direction from God, yet when David rebuked him, corrected him, and taught him, there was no argument from Abishai. The Abishai Anointing is always teachable.

Are you teachable? When you have a word, an idea, or a plan, can your leadership veto it and not offend you? The height of pride is to feel that you have been given the word for your church body even though that word contradicts God's appointed authority. The Abishai Anointing submits every word to God's leadership with the scriptural understanding that God works through His kingdom chain of command. If you cannot submit to that kind of correction, then you have either not found your David, or you need to repent and readjust your view of God's kingdom.

For years I prayed that I would meet David Wilkerson. This great man of God, pastor of Times Square Church in New York City, had always spoken powerfully to my heart through his messages. His books, *The Cross and the Switchblade*, *The Vision*, *Set the Trumpet to Thy Mouth* and *Have You Felt Like Giving Up Lately?* are Christian classics that brought me to my knees.

God answered my prayer, and I was invited to New York City for ministry at Times Square Church.

I felt this seasoned man of God would be a mentor for me. I was there to hear from God's man.

One night as I was with Bro. Dave, he asked me, "Denny, what do you want to do down in Shreveport? What is your vision?"

I shared several points of our vision as he nodded his head in approval. Then I said, "We feel God is leading us to start a Bible School."

He looked at me and said, "You don't need to start a Bible School. At your age, you haven't had enough experience to teach anybody anything yet, and you have no idea what is involved. A Bible school will take your focus off of what you need to be doing in other areas of ministry."

I was not offended! This is what I had prayed for and looked forward to – God's man speaking honestly into my life. I said, "I never thought of that. You are exactly right. We don't need to start a Bible school now."

What an advantage it is to walk without offense in relationship to the David anointing.

I am convinced the major reason men and women in today's church fall into error and are duped by what the word calls "clouds without rain" or "so much smoke," is they are not willing to receive correction. Every heresy has its beginning in the heart of an unteachable believer.

THE ABISHAI ANOINTING IS NEVER AFRAID TO STEP OUT AND SHARE A WORD FROM GOD, BUT AT THE SAME TIME IS WILLING TO RECEIVE TEACHING AND CORRECTION FROM THE DAVID ANOINTING.

What would happen in our churches if men and women of God walked in such trust that they were able to speak boldly into the lives of their comrades? Think of the unity, the power, and new anointing that teachable Abishais would bring.

8

ENGAGING THE GIANTS

AND Ishbi-Benob, one of the descendants of Rapha, whose bronze spearhead weighed three hundred shekels and who was armed with a new sword, said he would kill David.

But Abishai son of Zeruiah came to David's rescue; he struck the Philistine down and killed him. Then David's men swore to him, saying, "Never again will you go out with us to battle, so that the lamp of Israel will not be extinguished."

(II Samuel 21:16-17 NIV)

David was the warrior king. He did not send his troops into battle; he led them into the fray personally. In II Samuel 21, David fought a giant. Evidently Abishai positioned himself in battle so he could clearly see the king.

David was still a great warrior, but he did not have the stamina he once had. He suddenly became faint and passed out. In a flash Abishai was between David and the threat of the giant with his sword drawn. He then defeated the giant who would have destroyed the light of Israel.

I shared this message with a group of youth pastors and associates. As I began to talk about the Abishai Anointing engaging the giants in David's time of weakness, I saw tears fill the eyes of a young man sitting directly in front of me. After the session he approached me and said, "My pastor has been under attack physically. He has been so weak he hasn't been able to even attend church services." This young man then began to weep as he said, "My greatest joy in life has been to serve my pastor in his time of weakness."

The ABISHAI Anointing

When we genuinely love our leadership as we love ourselves, we are there for them in the seasons of life when they are faint, when the load is heavy, and when they are challenged emotionally, spiritually, or physically. We are there for them when their son is arrested or their young daughter gets pregnant. When mean Christians become the accuser's hit men, men and women with the Abishai Anointing engage the giants.

Countless men of God have fallen in battle with no Abishai to save them from the deadly spear of the giants of discouragement, burnout, and overwhelming crisis.

The Abishai Anointing engages the giants through sincere encouragement, faithfulness, loyalty, and warfare intercession. Every anointed man or woman of God will grow faint at some point. I pray in that moment that an Abishai is in close proximity.

9

THE KING,
NOT THE PALACE

AS King David approached Bahurim, a man from the same clan as Saul's family came out from there. His name was Shimei son of Gera, and he cursed as he came out.

He pelted David and all the king's officials with stones, though all the troops and the special guard were on David's right and left.

As he cursed, Shimei said, "Get out, get out, you man of blood, you scoundrel!

The LORD has repaid you for all the blood you

shed in the household of Saul, in whose place you have reigned. The LORD has handed the kingdom over to your son Absalom. You have come to ruin because you are a man of blood!"

Then Abishai son of Zeruiah said to the king, "Why should this dead dog curse my lord the king? Let me go over and cut off his head."

But the king said, "What do you and I have in common, you sons of Zeruiah? If he is cursing because the LORD said to him, 'Curse David,' who can ask, 'Why do you do this?'"

David then said to Abishai and all his officials, "My son, who is of my own flesh, is trying to take my life. How much more, then, this Benjamite! Leave him alone; let him curse, for the LORD has told him to.

It may be that the LORD will see my distress and repay me with good for the cursing I am receiving today."

So David and his men continued along the road while Shimei was going along the hillside opposite him, cursing as he went and throwing stones at him and showering him with dirt.

The king and all the people with him arrived at their destination exhausted. And there he refreshed himself.

(II Samuel 16:5-14 NIV)

Absalom, David's son, had led a coup that successfully removed David from the throne. David is once more running for his life. The king that ushered in Israel's Golden Age is now leaving by the back door of the palace. His own son seeks his throne, but his nephew Abishai seeks only his fellowship. Absalom loves the palace, but Abishai loves the king. As Abishai marched briskly beside David, barking commands to the others, he knew the great days in the palace were probably over. No more royal parties, buffets, and perks. No more autograph seekers as he and the other famous warriors marched through the marketplace. They were back where they started – fugitives with a price on their heads. It did not matter to Abishai though. His joy had never been the palace; it had always been the king.

Can you imagine the conversations that night? Where are we going? Back to Adullam? All the way to Philistia perhaps? It didn't matter, for wherever David went the action occurred. Few contemporary men and women have known that kind of camaraderie in the kingdom of God. I think, however, that all believers long for it.

One of Saul's relatives found the escape route that David and his men were using and began to curse the king and throw stones at him.

Abishai turned to David and said, *"Why should this dead dog curse my lord the king? Let me go over and cut off his head"* (II Samuel 16:9). To Abishai, David had always been the king. He had been the king at Adullam. He had been the king in the palace, and now he was the king in exile. The palace at Jerusalem did not make a great king out of David, but David made the palace of Jerusalem the glory of all the earth.

When the spiritual history of the decade of the 1990s is recorded, a prominent chapter will deal with the miracle of Promise Keepers and their remarkable leader Bill McCartney. I first met Coach McCartney in the early 1980s and didn't know he was a believer. A player on his Colorado Buffaloes team had gotten his permission to have me speak to the team one afternoon after practice.

I waited until practice was over and Coach McCartney had gathered his team for a few final instructions. He motioned to me to come and share with the players. As I walked toward the team, the Holy Spirit spoke clearly to me and said, "Speak exactly what I give you and don't worry about being invited back." I spoke for five minutes and gave a direct call for repentance and salvation. After closing in prayer, I walked quickly out the gate toward my car.

Coach McCartney called out to me, "Hey, Denny, wait a

minute." I will never forget his words to me, "Denny, I can't tell you how thankful I am for you coming and telling my team about being born again!" He went on to say something that took on much greater significance almost ten years later. He said, "God has called me to this campus, and I believe He is going to do something here that will speak to the entire nation."

Coach McCartney and I would become friends over the next few years. We had a time of fellowship each year at a conference for professional and college athletes in Phoenix, Arizona. When I began a high school football program at our Christian school in Shreveport, Louisiana, Coach McCartney consented to be our first banquet speaker.

Very early on I saw a prophetic anointing on this humble man of God. As he spoke of his love for Christ it was like laser light piercing the heart. Coach McCartney began to have great success as a head coach at Colorado University. His Buffaloes became one of the nation's marquee teams and even won a national championship.

because they taught that there is a missing anointing that is vital to the body of Christ. It is not the anointing of David who casts the vision, but rather, it is the anointing of an Abishai who empowers God's leader with love, loyalty, and commitment.

There are people who spend their whole lives defending brick, plaster, a steeple and an acre of ground, yet they never know the joy of empowering a David with an Abishai Anointing.

The Abishai Anointing is an extraordinary anointing which empowers ordinary men and women. It is born in tough times. It is an anointing that is always ready to go with the chosen man or woman of God, tackling impossible tasks. This anointing walks in covenant agreement with God's appointed leader, always displaying a teachable spirit, and engaging the giants when necessary. The Abishai Anointing loves the king, not the palace.

Is God calling you to the Abishai Anointing?

The ABISHAI Anointing

Our high school coaching staff made a visit to a Boulder clinic under Coach Mac and his great collection of coaches. That week is one that impacted our lives forever. On Friday, we were invited to Coach McCartney's home for dinner. On the way to his home, he told us about the blessing of God in providing his family with a new house. He said, "All I asked for myself was one room." I envisioned a trophy room sporting memorabilia from his illustrious career.

When we arrived, there really was a room where a few football memories and mementos were displayed. I thought this must be his room. But Coach Mac walked briskly past us and said, "Come on, let me show you my room." We walked a few steps down a hallway and turned right into a small room with only two pieces of furniture – an altar and a desk.

Coach McCartney said, "This is where I meet God every morning. This is where I cry out for God to touch the ministers of America."

Later that evening, Coach Mac shared with us the vision

of Promise Keepers. I could not even comprehend what he was saying! It was too big, too glorious, too new! He stated emphatically that God had shown him stadiums full of men worshipping God, men of every church background and every ethnic group throwing away their prejudice and pride at the foot of the cross. He spoke of his vision of one million men going to Washington, D.C., for a prayer meeting.

I have a very vivid picture of Coach McCartney kneeling at his personal altar in his special room, crying out for the pastors of America.

The vision of Bill McCartney was overwhelming, and of course, now all of it has become documented history. God has actually done exceedingly, abundantly above all even Coach McCartney could think or ask. Perhaps the most glorious part of the vision, however, was Coach McCartney's desire to see pastors healed and restored. Never in all of history has such a massive response of pastors to any organization occurred like it did with Promise Keepers.

I believe the reason Promise Keepers prospered is